I0005333

Raspberry Pi 3

*The Ultimate User Guide
to Getting Started with
Raspberry Pi 3*

Table of Contents

© Copyright 2017 by Lifestyle Initiative, Inc. - All rights reserved.

The follow eBook is reproduced below with the goal of providing information that is as accurate and reliable as possible. Regardless, purchasing this eBook can be seen as consent to the fact that both the publisher and the author of this book are in no way experts on the topics discussed within and that any recommendations or suggestions that are made herein are for entertainment purposes only. Professionals should be consulted as needed prior to undertaking any of the action endorsed herein.

This declaration is deemed fair and valid by both the American Bar Association and the Committee of Publishers Association and is legally binding throughout the United States.

Furthermore, the transmission, duplication or reproduction of any of the following work including specific information will be considered an illegal act irrespective of if it is done electronically or in print. This extends to creating a secondary or tertiary copy of the work or a recorded copy and is only allowed with express written consent from the Publisher. All additional right reserved.

The information in the following pages is broadly considered to be a truthful and accurate account of facts and as such any inattention, use or misuse of the information in question by the reader will render any resulting actions solely under their purview. There are no scenarios in which the publisher or the original author of this work can be in any fashion deemed liable for any hardship or damages that may befall them after undertaking information described herein.

Additionally, the information in the following pages is intended only for informational purposes and should thus be thought of as universal. As befitting its nature, it is presented without assurance regarding its prolonged validity or interim quality. Trademarks that are mentioned are done without written consent and can in no way be considered an endorsement from the trademark holder.

Introduction

Congratulations on downloading *Raspberry Pi 3: The Ultimate User Guide to Getting Started with Raspberry Pi 3* and thank you for doing so.

The following chapters will discuss everything that you need to know in order to get started with the Raspberry Pi 3. This is one of the best products that you are able to use when it is time to learn a new coding language or when you are looking for a way to introduce yourself to some great computer sciences without having to worry about it being too complicated. This guidebook will provide you with the steps that are needed to get the right Pi device and to make sure that it is working inside of all your projects.

Inside this guidebook, we are going to start out with some of the basics of working with the Raspberry Pi 3 and what it is all about, including some of the benefits. Then we will move on to how to get the operating system to work on this device (there isn't one included so you have the freedom to make the choices that you would like), as well as getting this system to boot up. We will also spend some time talking about the Python coding language and how to use it before you get started on any of your projects.

Once we know some of the basics, it is time to move on to creating some of the great projects that are promised with this board. There are so many things that you are able to do with the Raspberry Pi 3 and since it is such an inexpensive board, you will be able to try out many of them. Some of the things that we are going to use this board for includes making our own home automation system and creating a gaming console.

When you are ready to learn a bit more about the Raspberry Pi 3 and see what cool projects you are able to do, this guidebook is the tool that you need to get it all done.

There are plenty of books on this subject on the market, thanks again for choosing this one! Every effort was made to ensure it is full of as much useful information as possible, please enjoy!

Chapter 1: Learning About the Raspberry Pi 3

The world of coding languages and computer sciences can be a great one to get into. You will be able to learn about them in order to know more about how your computer works and even how to create some of your own projects. You can make decisions about which coding language you want to go with, what operating system will help you to get this done the best, and you can even choose to work with single board computers, such as Raspberry Pi 3, to make robotics projects, and you can have a lot of fun in the process. Too many times we believe that we aren't able to learn coding and have fun with it because it is too technical and hard to learn; but with the right project and the right mindset, you are going to be able to make so much happen.

The best single board computer to go with, no matter what kind of projects you are going to do with it, is the Raspberry Pi 3. This one has all the power that you need, especially when you compare it with a regular personal computer, but it is much smaller and has an affordable price tag at just $35. Once we get into some of the projects that are possible with the Raspberry Pi 3, you will wonder why you didn't have one before.

When developers first started to work on the Raspberry Pi 3, they designed it to help out in classrooms that were learning coding and computer sciences. This device is great for this idea if you are in the process of learning coding, but for the most part, a new audience has taken over; those who are interested in taking the single board computer and using it for their own robotics and electronics projects.

The Raspberry Pi 3 is going to come with all the accessories that you need in order to plug it into the computer, control how it works, add in a keyboard and a mouse, and so much more. You do need to find some third party distributors in order to find these attachments, but you can add on a lot of parts that you need to keep the board running smoothly. As you will see in this guidebook, these attachments can be used to help you to make the Raspberry Pi 3 board into a gaming console a media center, and so much more.

Why would I use the Raspberry Pi 3?

For someone who is just getting started with computer sciences and trying to figure out which board you would like to go with, there are many options and you may be curious as to why the Raspberry Pi 3 is the best option for your needs. There are many benefits to going with this device and some of these benefits include:

- Work with coding in Python: when it comes to beginners learning a new coding language, Python is the best one to use. It is based off the English language and is written to be easy to read and understand. This is the main language that you are able to use inside of the Raspberry Pi 3. If you know one of the other languages, such as C++ or Java, these are preprogrammed inside of the device so you are able to use those as well.

- As a good operating system: the Raspbian operating system is easy to work with and with the projects in this guidebook, you will learn all of the different uses that you can do with it. Since it is designed to work specifically with the Raspberry Pi device, you have all the options you need to get the project up and running.

- This device is convenient to work with: the Raspberry Pi 3 is one of the most convenient tools that you are able to use for your robotic project needs. This board is small so you are able to take it with you. You can use it to work on a variety of projects, with all the versatility that you need to make your projects, bit or small, work properly.

- Helps you to learn about computer sciences: remember that the original reason that this little computer was developed was to help you to learn more about computer sciences and coding. This device is perfect for getting this done. You are able to learn how to code with the Python language on it, learn the right codes to make a brand new project (and there are many of them that you are able to work with), and so much more.

These are just a few of the benefits that you will be able to find when you are working with the Raspberry Pi 3. It is a great single board computer that is going to bring some of your projects to life and it has all the power that you need, along with the simplicity, so that even beginners feel comfortable using this computer on their own.

Getting the Raspberry Pi 3 to Boot Up

Now that we have spent some time talking about the Raspberry Pi 3, it is time to get to work and make sure that it boots up and works the right way. Take the device and try to turn it on. The first time that you try to turn this device, you will probably notice that the operating system is not even there. You will need to do the work to install it onto an SD card and then move it so that it works on the Raspberry Pi 3, but the device is not going to come with this already placed on it. This means that you will need to go through a couple of extra steps in order to get the Raspberry Pi 3 to work the way that you would like, but you do get a bit more freedom in choosing which operating system that you would like to work with.

Unlike working with the personal laptop that you are used to, the Raspberry Pi 3 works with a processor that is considered an ARM processor.

This can get pretty complex, but what is pretty much means is that there are some programs that you can't do with this device that you can with your regular personal computer, so it is important to pick out an operating system that works to complete the tasks that you want. The Linux operating system has one that is specifically meant for the Raspberry Pi products, the Raspbian operating system, and this is the one that we will use on the programs that we do inside this guidebook.

There are some other great operating systems that you are able to use when it comes to getting the Raspberry Pi 3 set up, but the Raspbian is one of the best for you to use because of all the great features that are on it and the fact that it is designed to specifically work with these products.

So once you have chosen the type of operating system that you would like to use with your system, it is time to pick out the Raspberry Pi that you want to work with and bring out an SD card. You will need to download the newest version of the operating system onto the SD card so that you are able to move it over to the Raspberry Pi and get it to work properly. The Raspbian operating system is free so outside of the items that we just listed, you will not need to bring along any other tools.

So, bring up the latest version of the Raspbian operating system onto your personal computer and then download it. This will take a few minutes so have some patience to make it happen. Once this is downloaded, you can go over to the right file and then look for the portion that says "extract all" and click on it. This part is important because it is going to help to extract out the file image so that you can download it and get it to work right on the Raspberry Pi device.

Now, this is just one of the steps that you will be doing in order to get the operating system downloaded on to your Pi device. You will also need to download a program that can take this operating system information that you place onto the SD card and get it so that you would be able to use it on the Pi device. There are a few options for this, but one of the best (and the one that we are going to use), is the Win32DishImager, which is another free option that you can work with. Take some time to let this download as well and then move it to the SD card. You will then be able to click on the Extract All that we talked about to make sure that the program works.

With the programs that we are using, we will not need to do an installation. You will be able to start it without waiting by clicking onto your file. You should also make sure that when you are starting to move the operating system over, you pick out an SD card that is empty so that there is enough room to go with. once you start, the Wheezy file image is one of the best ones to pick and you will just need to move it over to the location where the SD card is held; you should be careful when looking about where to put this so that you are able to find it later and it doesn't go to the wrong place.

Once you are into the file of the SD card, you will need to press Write. This part does take a bit because you are moving the operating system to the card at this point. While you are waiting, add in the mouse and the keyboard that you would like to use with the system inside and any other attachments that you want with the Pi device as well as connecting this to a monitor or a television.

Time for the first boot

Once you have had some time to move all of your operating system over to the SD card, you will need to take it out of your personal computer and place it into the Pi device. At this point, the Pi device should have all the right components besides the power supply plugged in right. You will now need to take the device and get it plugged into the source of power. Watch the monitor screen or your TV screen and see if the boot sequence is showing up or not. After this first boot, you will notice that the device is going to boot up right into the setup mode. If your device isn't inside the setup mode, you may need to try and get it to do another boot to end up there.

It is a good idea to take a bit of time to work through the settings so that you can make some changes on the Pi device. For example, some of the things that you are able to change inside the device includes the speed of the pictures, how big the screen is, the volume, and more. You are able to go back to settings later on if it is needed, but it may be a good idea to change at least a few of the settings right now.

At this point, the operating system should be ready to go as long as you moved the SD card over to the Pi device. This is going to make it easier for you to start using the device and work on some of the projects that you would like.

Learning a coding language

This is a type of computer that we are dealing with, which means that you will need to work with a coding language in order to get the programs to work and to tell the program how you would like to get it to work. There are actually several coding languages you can work with on the Raspberry Pi 3, so this does make it quite a bit easier to work with.

For the most part, when you are working with the Raspberry Pi 3, you will want to work with the Python coding language. This is one of the easiest coding languages that you can work with and it is pretty much designed for beginners. For those who have never worked in coding in the past and don't know any of the languages, this is probably the best one to go with because it is perfect for the beginner.

Now, there are a few other coding languages that you are able to use when it comes to the Raspberry Pi three. Perl, Java, and C++ are some of the most common ones that are already preprogrammed inside of the Pi device and if you already know how to use any of these languages, you will be able to bring them up and get the device to still work. You get some freedom in the coding language that you will use on this device so go ahead and pick the ones that you like the best out of all of them.

And that is all that you need to do in order to get the Raspberry Pi 3 up and running. By this point you should have the operating system working on the device and you can learn a coding language (or work with one that you already know), as we work through this guidebook and do some of the projects that are there.

Chapter 2: Configuring Your Raspberry Pi 3

The developers who have worked on the Raspberry Pi 3 have worked hard in order to become one of the premier options on the market as the best software platform when it comes to developing your own robotics projects or for those who are learning how to work in computer sciences. When you take the time to compare it to a few of the other similar computers that are available, you will notice that the Pi devices are some of the best because they are really easy to work with, they have the ability to work with many different operating systems, and there is the option to work on many different projects.

But while there are quite a few things that you are going to be able to do with these devices, you first need to make sure that you are familiar with how the Raspbian system works before you work on any projects. You will need to know how to turn on the device, change some of the settings on the device, and more.

The first thing we can concentrate on in this is learning how to configure the device. The platform for the Raspbain operating system is the one that we use for the projects in this guidebook because you will be able to use the distro of Debian, which is through Linux, and it is made to work with the Pi devices. It is not going to have quite as much power as you are used to when working on your personal computer and the operating system that is on there, but the Pi device is much smaller and if you tried to put one of these bigger operating systems on it, you would be disappointed by how slow it all is.

The Raspbian operating system is one of the best for your Pi device because it has quite a bit of power behind it, but it is still small and compact enough to work inside the Pi device without slowing things down at all. But most of us have not worked with this operating system in the past, so it is hard to know where things are, what we are able to do with the operating system to get the most out of it, or how it works.

When you open up the operating system, there is going to be a menu that pops up when installing the software, but if you happened to try and bypass this step or didn't do it the first time that you installed this, it is important to take care of this now. You will simply need to type in "sudo raspi-configu" in order to proceed to the next step.

Now remember that this is going to be a bit slower than you are used to working with so you may need to wait a bit before the menu comes and shows up on the screen. Once this screen shows up, you will be able to work with the arrows that are there in order to navigate the options and pick which of them you want to work with. Once the option that you would like is selected, just press the Enter key and follow through all the menu options. You should notice that there are quite a few that you can pick from so take some time to learn what they are all able to do before moving on.

When you are working on getting this configured, you will need to go through the settings a bit and get things to set up the way that you would like. For the most part this is going to all set up the way that you would like, but if you find that some issues are coming up, you should work with the Graphic User Interface, or the GUI, (you can get to this with the start command). Sometimes you will be able to fix some of these common errors simply by having Pi do a reboot once or twice so that all the updates will come through. Also, with the operating system being a bit slower on the Pi device than you are used to, you may just need to sit back and let it do its work before jumping to conclusions about it not working.

Adding some security to the Raspberry Pi 3

While you should take some time in the beginning of owning this device to do the configuration to help this to work the proper way, it is also a good idea for you to spend some time making sure that the Pi device is as secure as possible. Sometimes beginners are going to get confused because they forget that this is actually a computer system that can get viruses and other things that you can get just like with your personal computer. This means that you will need to take some time to make sure that the Pi device is protected from threats and other issues that come up throughout your time with the device.

It is also important that you make sure that every installation for your updates are done properly to avoid some issues. If you want to skip this step, you will find that the external threats can come onto the system, especially when you are trying to download some of the things that you need for these projects. It is a good idea for you to secure the device a bit before you ever take it online to get some things for the different projects.

To make sure that you are getting the Pi device is secure as possible includes using the raspi_config tool and going to this menu. Then you can open it up and write down the commands that are below:

Sudo apt-get update
Sude apt-get upgrade

These are going to help you to get the updates and security that you would like to keep the program working well, but keep in mind that the processing power is lower than the others that you are used to, even compared to the power that is on your smartphone, sot eh installation is going to take you a bit longer to get done. Just give it the time that you need before going online and getting any new software or tools that you need.

By the time you get these codes all done and into the system, you will have a device that is secure with the settings that you would like to use. You are going to find that this is a really great product for you to work with because it is inexpensive (at only $35 for the most part), but it is also going to be set up to help you to get your coding done, to learn a bit more about computer sciences, and to even do some of your own computer projects. While there are some limitations to what you will be able to do with this, there are still many options that you will love when working on this device.

Chapter 3: Some of the Guidelines That Are Needed to Ensure the Raspberry Pi Projects Goes Well

So when most people choose to work with the Raspberry Pi, they are interested in it because they have heard about lots of good projects that they are able to do with the help of this device. You may already have a few projects that you would like to use on this device and you want to get the operating system all loaded up and ready to go. While we did spend some time configuring the system, making sure that it is secure, and downloading the operating system, it is time to work on how to create some of the projects that you want by learning some of the guidelines.

The first part of this that you will work on it to learn about some of the components that will make the project work. There are a lot of great attachments that you are able to add into this project, but we are going to take a look at the minimum that you will need with the Pi device to see what will make it work. At a minimum, you are going to be able to see that a mouse, a keyboard, a memory card, some of the software, and a way to get the information that will tell the program what to do. Luckily you are able to reuse some of the same components with the different projects that you would like to work on.

If you are uncertain about which components that you will need in order to work on your project and which ones are going to work the best with your version of the Raspberry Pi 3, you can always go and check out the Raspberry Pi website. Most of these attachments are going to be made by third party manufacturers and not by the Raspberry Pi team so you will need to read some reviews and double check in order to find out which ones work on the device you are using.

When you are ready to get started on a project, there are several things that you should keep in mind to make sure that the project is going to work the way that you would like including:

- When you are ready to start on the project, you need to make sure that you have a pretty good idea of what you want to have happen when you get to the end of the project. With this in mind, it is easier to have an idea of what items you would need and you can ensure that the project goes the right way from the start.
- You will need to make sure that the device is going to make it possible to reach the results at the end.
- Are you going to use this device in order to compile and send you a list of all sensory results from this projects?
- Based on whatever project you are working on, will the Pi device send you the results that it finds or will it just move

over to the proceeding results without an direction from you.

- If you choose to make sure that the device is going to send out notifications, what is the method that you would like to use in order to send this out.

- What signal are you going to be using for the output?

- What are some of the peripherals that you will need in order to make sure that the right output is sent out.

- Is there a particular coding language that you would need to be able to use to make it easier to work on the project?

Before you get started on any of the projects that you would like to work with, it is a good idea for you to answer some of these questions so that you know what is going to happen from the beginning all the way to the end.

So, if you would like to make sure that the Pi device is going to work the right way for you. We are going to take some time to look through these questions by creating one of our first projects. We will talk about a few more of these later on, but first we will start out with just this one to see how the questions are going to work on this. The first project that we are trying to work with is to create a Home Automation system, that will be able to help you recognize when a person or another animal is by the door of your house and the information is going to be sent over to your phone. There are quite a few ways that you will be able to make this project work, but we will make this a simple as possible and walk you through some of the steps that are needed.

Going through the questions on this first project

Now, going back to some of the questions that we were asking at the beginning of this, we will need to use those in order to figure out the answers of them to work on the project. First, the question that we need to ask is how we are going to be able to use the board with the Raspberry Pi in order to make this project work the right way. The Pi device is one of the best options because you are able to use it in order to sense any motion that is by your door, plus it can be set up to send out the signal about this information to a smartphone, as long as you are using the right codes with it.

The next question that you are going to need to ask is whether the device is going to be able to compile a list of the sensory results that you get. With this particular project, yes, the Pi device will be able to collect all of this information concerning the motion that is sensed by your door. We are going to use what is called the PIR sensor in order to help this out and you will need to hook this up to some light that you keep on outside the door. Then when the sensor notices that there is a bit of obstruction to your light, such as what will happen when something walks to the door, you will be able to get this information that someone is there.

The next question that you will be able to ask is whether you are going to be receiving this information or not. With this case, you are going to be using the Pi computer in order to send the information out to you when someone comes to the door. This is also going to be an answer to the following question on the list because you are going to learn where this information is sent. When we are working on this project, we are going to use our smartphone in order to receive information about the signal.

And now that we have the information about the other questions, you will need to work on the peripherals that the program need in order to make the new project work the way that you would like. First, it is important to work with a relay network board since this is the one that you use in order to power up the board and external circuitry that you will use. The PIR sensor is important too because it is in charge of finding the movement that you want and it works well next to a light because you will need to obstruct that in order to get the results. An SD card is also good because you will need to have the Raspbian operating system on it as well as an Ethernet cable (it is always better to go with this to keep the internet connection as steady as possible).

Once you have all your questions answered about the board, and you have taken some time to go and get the items that are needed for this project, you will need to use these steps below in order to get the motion detector all set up and ready to go:

- Bring out the Raspberry Pi 3 board that you are going to want to use, as well as the peripherals and attachments that we talked about earlier.

- You first need to make sure that you set up a plan so that you are able to get all of the pins assigned in the right place. You need to remember that when using your sensor, it is going to have its own source of power and it is going to have an earth pin.

- Taking the time to get the pins in the right order is important as well. You will find that using the 40 pin matrix is the easiest way to work with the pins and get them all set up.

- So, the peripheral ones need to be done first. Look at the two pins that are over by you 5V power source as well as the ground. There should also be 4 pins that are saved for the output and the input on the Pi board.

- Once those are done, it is time for you to try to get the PIR sensor to work. You will be responsible for setting it up so that there are three minutes for the ground and the power and then just 1 that will work for the sensory output.

- Once the wires are in place for this one you can work on connecting the light sensor. You can use 2 different pins to make this one happen. These are going to be near the 3V and then you will need to have a pin that goes from the sensor over to the sensory output.

- Now it is time to connect the GSM module with your two pins that are being used for the power and with the one that works with the output. If you are confused on how this is supposed to look, you can use the plan outlay to help you.

- Once you have placed all the pins above, take the memory card that is holding your Raspbian operating system and place it into the Pi device. Connect this to the internet using the Ethernet cord, and then place the USB port inside so that the boar can be hooked to a power source.

- Take the time to boot the board up and let it connect with your computer. Once this has happened, it is time to open up the R Pi Home+ software (or you can use any other browser that works the best for your need). You need to do this so that you can find the IP address for the device.

- Take the time to put in the password and username on this device and then configure the pins properly. You may also take this time to change up some of the settings.

- To do this, take the time to click on settings. See what the GPIO pin settings are before you start to Edit. Clicking on Edit will lead you right to where these 40 pins are listed out on the page.

- Take a look and find out which pin you are using for the light sensor. You are going to need to make some changes to this one in order to make the input digital. You can also take some time to rename this to Light sensor to make it easier to find. Take the time to save these changes so that they actually stick.

- You are able to go back through and redo some of these steps with the help of the PIR sensor, but you would need to do the output state instead of the digital input that we just did. Make sure that you do this with all three of the outputs from your relay network.

- After you have done these changes, it is going to lead you over to the home page. Here you can notice that there is a list of inputs and outputs that are on display.

- At this point, you should go to the selection page for I/O and configure what kind of output that you will use. You can also turn the task for the light sensor so that they start to rely on the motion sensing of the PIR.

- You can then repeat these steps a few times until you get all the inputs and outputs to work the right way for this project.

While there are a few steps that you will need to take in order to make this happen, when you are done you will be able to do some experimenting in order to see how the project is going to work. For this part, hold on to the computer in your hand and then move in front of the light sensor. If you see that the LED light is blinking, you know that this project is successful and that it is trying to record the motions that you are doing.

The device should be up and running at this point. Now it is up to you to find the right location to place this item so that it is able to record the motions that are going on and to ensure that the data is going to you the right way. The device is now set up to help you to record all the motion that comes near your door and you will be able to get the homepage to send the information over to you to get it to work properly and so you can monitor who is coming to your house.

This is just the simple form of the project and there is so much that you can choose to do if you want to expand out the project and get it to do more. For example, you could take the time to add on a camera so that you get pictures of the people or animals who are trying to come up to the door. You can change it so that the locks are connected to each other so that if you see a family member is trying to get into the house, you can use your phone in order to take care of this. You can move this over to the garage door to have that open and shut when you need it and so much more. This is a device that you can use all around the house to make it into a smart house if needed without having to spend quite as much money on the work.

At this point, you are all done with the work that you need in order to make your own home automation system. It was a simple project (and we will talk about some more later on), that can help you to get the feel for how the Raspberry Pi 3 works and all the cool things that you will be able to do with this device. Try it out and see if the device works out the right way for your needs.

Chapter 4: How to Make the Programming Work Inside the Raspberry Pi 3

We mentioned this one a bit before, but you do have the option to choose the programming language that you would like to use when you deal with the Raspberry Pi 3. There are several programming languages that are installed onto this device so you have some choices, but since it is mostly beginners who are working on these projects, they will all usually pick to go with the Python code. The Python coding language is easy to work with, it has a simple language setup that you will love, it is designed to work for beginners without being too complex, and it works on the Linux operating system.

The Python language has always been one of the better ones to choose because it is designed with the beginner in mind. There is a lot of power behind what you can do with the Python language, but you also get to combine this with a simple syntax that most people can learn pretty quickly. If you are in this part of the book, we have already had a few examples of Python code earlier in this book so you can see that it is not that complicated. You are also able to take the Python coding language and get it to work across many operating systems and the instructions have become even easier to use when working on the Pi device so you can bring this language wherever you would like.

While we have spent some time talking about some of the projects that you are able to do with the Raspberry Pi 3 and all the cool things this board is able to 0, it is also a good idea to spend some time learning about the Python programming language so that you understand what is going on with this language and how to use it with the different projects that you would like. We are going to take a look at some of the basics that come with the Python coding language, such as decision making, basic operators, lists, modules, functions, loops, and some of the other neat things that you will want to learn how to use to make the Python language do what you want on the Raspberry Pi 3.

What is the big deal about Python?

When you are looking for a coding language that has a lot of power and features behind it, but you are worried about figuring this language out because you are a beginner, the Python coding language is the right one for you. Python is a general purpose language which means that you can use it on a variety of projects as you would like, but it is sill easy enough for the beginner to learn about.

You are also going to like that the Python program is really interactive to work with. You are able to use it to develop a variety of situations, including some where you are able to ask he questions and then get the answer based on what output the code gives you. You can also combine it together with a few of the other coding languages, such as C++, if you want to make sure that it is able to hold on to enough power to get things done or if you want to try out something completely new.

Different types of programming

Whenever you decide to work with the Python program, there are a few programming types that you will get familiar with. The first one that you may spend some time with is the interactive mode programming. This one is going to try to invoke an interpreter by passing on a command to read and then it will look into the code to see where the instructions are. It is going to be based on the codes that you are putting into the system ad it will print off (or show on the screen) the information that you ask for.

The second type of programming that you may have to work with inside of Python is the script mode programming. This one is going to ask you to invoke the interpreter based on the script parameter, and then it will execute the whole length of your script, going until it finally gets to the end of the program. We will assume with this one that there are no mistakes and that the Python interpreter is able to get through the whole program when it makes the output that you want.

Working with your identifiers

When we are talking about a coding language, even if it's another one besides Python, the identifiers are going to be the words that you or your user are able to define. They can be many different parts of the Python code including variables, functions, constants, classes, and modules. You will be able to also choose the characters that you are using with this one, going with a letter that is either lower case or upper case, an underscore symbol, or a number. Other special characters are not allowed when naming the identifier because this is just going to make the system confused. And while numbers are allowed in the name, you should never use them as the first character in the name; you can place them in anywhere else that you would like.

Also take note of the reserved words and do not use these as ways to name your identifier. There are may words that are reserved in the Python language and they are meant to tell the compiler what you would like to get done. They are basically commands for the compiler an if you are using them incorrectly and having them as names of your identifiers, you are basically going to confuse the system. For example, if you decided to use the word "print" as the name of one of your identifiers, the compiler would assume that it is supposed to type out the information that comes after the word print, and you could have a mess in the code.

The comments inside of Python

There are some times when you are writing out a code when you need to leave a little note for the other programmers or use it as a way to better explain what is going on inside of your code. You will be able to leave some comments inside the code and when you use the right symbols, you will be able to do this without confusing the compiler or sending out the wrong message on the code. These are really easy to do and you are able to add on as many as you would like, although you should probably keep it to a minimum or you could end up with a messy looking code. If you would like to leave a little comment inside of the code to make sure others know what you are doing or to answer questions that may come up inside of your work, you should just need to use the (//) sign. Any time that the compiler sees this, it is going to just skip over it and look for the next part of the code.

The operators inside of Python

Another addition to your code that you will find interesting is the idea of operators. These are good to know how to use because they are going to add in some functionality to the code that you are working on. There are several different kinds of operators that you are able to work with inside the code. For example, you would want to work with the arithmetic operators any time that you need to do some addition, subtraction, or another mathematical equation inside of your ode. Or you could work on the assignment operators in order to provide a value with your variable and to keep things organized. Or you can use the comparison operators if you are taking two pieces of code and trying to see if they are the same or not.

What are the classes in Python?

When you want to make sure that your code is as organized and nice looking as possible, you will want to learn how to work with classes. These classes are like storage containers that are going to hold all of the similar objects of a code together. This will make it a bit easier for you to find things that you need later on and you will be able to recognize all the different parts that are inside.

The objects that you are placing into the containers, or the classes, that you are working with should all have some similarities in order to make sense for them to be together. The objects don't have to be exactly the same in order to fit into the same class, but others should be able to look into the class and notice that these are similar and recognize why these are put together they way that they are.

Adding in the loops

There are several times in your coding when you will decide that it is a good idea to add in a loop. When you use the loop, you are going to make the code repeat the same block of information over and over again. Sometimes you are going to do it so that the loop continues until you turn off the device and other times you will want to add in the loop to just go off a certain amount of times (such as 20) before it stops. The loops will help you to do this as many times as you want without having to write out the code a million times to make this work.

There are a lot of parts that come into play when you are working on the Python language. These are just some of the simple ones that you can bring up in order to learn how to work in the language and to make sure that it is going to give you the results that you want while working on the Raspberry Pi board. Some of the codes are going to be simple, like some of the ones that we showed earlier in this book, and some are going to be a bit more complex and will use several of the parts that we talked about. Either way, the Python code is still simple to work with even when you add in lots of parts, and it is simply a way for you to make the code more powerful.

Looking at some examples of Python code.

Now that we have learned about some of the simple parts that come with the Python code, it is time to take a look at how the code is going to look when you take it and write it out on the Raspberry Pi 3 device. You are going to need to use the Python code in order to make the projects work that we will design in this book, and many of them are going to have the same syntax and more to make things happen. Here is a good example of the Python code and how it is going to work in order to program the GPI pins.

#blink.py //opens the file containing the instructions
Import RPi.GPIO as GPIO //sets the default instructions to include the GPI port
> *Import time //Used to keep time*
> *GPIO.setmode(GPIO.BOARD)*
> *GPIO.setup(7, GPIO.OUT)*
> *While true:*

```
GPIO.output(7, Ture)
Time.sleep(0.2)
GPIO.outut(7, False)
Time.sleep (0, 2)
```

Once you have taken the time to type this into the compiler, you will see that it is short, but has some good information inside of it. The idea behind this one is that you are trying to make the LED light work by having it blink for you. In the first part of this code, you are going to be working with the pin 7 in order to make it initialize. Then we are going to work on a while loop, which is inside of the code, so that the blinking happens more than once. All of this is simply going to start as soon as the program sees that your statement of blink.py is considered true. Whenever the information is seen as false, the light is going to turn off for about .2 seconds before turning back on (because the statement is true again) for .2 seconds as well.

We do not have a break part inside of this code in order to make the blinking stop on its own. This basically means that you are going to see the LED light continue to blink on and off at the right intervals until you turn the device off. If you would like to have this only blink a certain amount of times, you will be able to change up the code a bit and tell it just how any times the light needs to bling in order to make this work properly.

And that is all there is to working with the Python code. We will have some more examples of how to write out this code later on and we work on some more projects, but this gives you a good idea about how it all works and helps you to see that this is a simple language that you can work with even as a beginner. With a bit of practice and trying out some of the other projects that are available, you are going to be able to do so much with the Python language and get some amazing results to help you out.

Chapter 5: Creating Your Own Home Arcade Box

Now that we have spent some time learning more about the ideas that are behind the Raspberry Pi 3 and how to make it work with the Python language (you can also choose to go with some of the other coding languages if you are more comfortable with them), it is time to start working on some of the projects that you are able to complete with the help of this system. With this particular project, we are going to work in order to create your own at home arcade box. This box is not going to have the power to hold on to some of your newer games that you may use with some of the other arcade boxes, it is able to work with some of the older games that you used to love and it can still be a lot of fun.

You are most likely going to need to use an emulator in order to make these games work the best, and you will be able to pick out the one that you like the best by looking online. You can do this with several different consoles to make it work with the Raspberry Pi 3, such as the PlayStation PC, the Sega Genesis, or the SNES. Though most people will choose to work on the Raspbian operating system when they would like to make these games work on the Raspberry Pi 3, you can find that working on the RetroPie option is the best because it is designed for these kinds of games and it will help to make up some custom disk image so that you can enjoy the older titles.

What a lot of people like about making this project is that they are able to get the device to work almost exactly alike to the gaming boxes that are on the market. Yes, you will find that some of the newer games will not work on the device, but considering this one is just $35 and then you just need a few accessories to play the game, you could get away with a cheap version of playing some of your favorite games rather than spending hundreds on a brand new system.

Now, for those who would like to get started on this project and who would like to make sure that they are getting all of the parts in place to make your very own gaming console, there are going to be a few parts that you need to have on hand to get this to work. Some of the supplies that you need for this includes:

A TV

Some kind of HDMI cable

Your SD card (make sure that this is able to hold no less than 4GB.

The Raspberry Pi device that you want to use

Your power supply to turn it on.

If you would like to make it easier to play some of the games, you can consider a game controller.

With this project, when you are going through and picking out the right accessories that will go with this new gaming console, you should double check to see if they are going to be compatible with the Raspberry Pi device. The developers of Raspberry Pi do not create their own accessories to go with the device so you will need to search through the third party manufacturers to see what you can find and this sometimes gets a bit confusing and challenging.

Once you have taken the time to find your own supplies, it is time to bring out the RetroPie stuff and get it over to your SD card for the Pi. This is one of the best additions you can use if you would like to get some of these games ready to play with. You will be able to get this information by visiting https://retropie.org.uk/download and then pick out the version of the Raspberry Pi you are working with. This is another one that you will need to give some time before you move on to the net step. Just like with the operating system, you are going to need to use the Win32DiskImager in order to extract the image over to the SD card.

Now it is time to take the Raspberry Pi device and get it to boot up. As this is happening, take the device and get it all plugged in to the controller that you would like to use as well as to the computer you are using. Place the SD card inside and allow this to boot up. If you worked with everything properly, you should see that something known as the EmulationStation is going to pop up on the screen and you can take this time to configure the settings on the controller you want to play with. You should go through all the prompts and get it set up the right way at this time since it is the first time playing on this project.

Once you have some time to set up your controller, it is time to use this controller to make the next few parts a bit easier. You are able to use these in order to pilot through your emulators and get the RetroPie stuff all hooked up. You can also stop to set up the hot keys that will make this easier to do if you would like. Once you have the proper controller set up and

ready to go, make sure to save the work you have
done and then get out of this part of the process.

The next step for you to work on is to make sure
that the program is going to work with your Wi-
Fi. Usually you are going to keep this on an
Ethernet cord, but since it is something simple
like games that will already be on the Pi device,
the Wi-Fi is going to be just fine. Using the
controller to make things a bit easier, you will
need to scroll on down so that you find the
section that is called Configure Wi-Fi. Use the
action button to click on this and once you get
that far, you will need to work on the Set Up
network. Look through the list of available
networks and decide which one is from your
home and that you would like to do.

Once the device has gotten the Wi-Fi that it
needs (you may need to use a password
depending on the settings that you are using on
the internet access), it is time to make the ROMs
move over to the Pi. This is a simple process, but

you will need to double check that the internet connection is strong or consider using the Ethernet cables to make this work. If your main computer is a Windows one, you can open up inside of the file manager and type in the code "//retropie". For those who are using a Mac computer for this, you need to go through and open your finder, select on Go, and then select on Connect to Server. You can type in the code "smb://retropie." These are going to work in the same way, but they make sure that your respective computer is doing the right work.

Now that everything is connected, it is time to transfer over the ROMS from the personal computer to the Raspberry Pi 3 device, going through the process remotely, which means that you are going to send the stuff over to the Pi without having it stuck to the computer this whole time. You can choose to bring over as many of these ROMS as you would like (as long as the SD card you are using is big enough to hold all that) or you can just go with a few games that you really want to work with.

Once all of the ROMs that you would like to work with are over onto the Pi device, it is time to reboot the device. Make sure to keep the controller plugged in during this time to keep things simple and to ensure that it is ready to go as soon as the reboot is done.

If you would like, you are able to just transfer the ROMs over directly to the Raspberry Pi device and just play them in this way. This one will save you some steps and make it easier, but you do need to remember that the Pi device has really limited storage space so with the operating system, you may only be able to get a few of these games onto it. If you would like to hold onto quite a few of these games, you are able to choose to move them over to an SD card or USB drive so that you can play as many of the games as you would like.

At this point, the Raspberry Pi 3 is all set up so that you are able to play some of your favorite older games on it. You are able to sit back and enjoy just one or two of the games or you can have a whole card filled with the fun ones that you want to play. Some of these are going to work a bit better than others, but remember that you are able to mess with the settings to help get some of them to work a little bit better.

Chapter 6: How to Make Your Own Phone with the Raspberry Pi 3

The phone market is always going through the roof. People want to make sure that they have a really reliable phone that will help them to get their work done and call people when they really need to, but many times the cost of the phone is going to be high. Phone companies are always asking hundreds of dollars for a new phone, and require you to get an expensive plan with them as well. And it never helps that the new phones are coming out every few months so you can never keep up with all the new things that are coming out.

If you are someone who would like to have a nice phone that works well without having to spend hundreds of dollars to keep up with the newest additions, this project is a good option for you to work with. You will just need a few supplies and the Raspberry Pi 3 and you can create one of your own phones. This could cost you less than $100 to do and it will be much easier to use, have the features that you want, and is sure to be more durable than you will find with some of the other phones you have recently purchased.

Making a phone with the help of the Raspberry Pi 3 is pretty easy and you are only going to need a few supplies to help this get started. For the most part, a GSM module is needed as well as a touch screen that can go on the Pi device and a battery pack. There are a few other things to keep it all put together without it falling apart, but you will already have some of the hardware requirements there. There are also some apps on the market, or even a specific software if you have one in mind for this and you can even add on an app file that will run with your smartphone.

This project is going to take a bit longer to complete than some of the others that we have discussed in this guidebook, but it is pretty easy considering how you are going to create your own phone out of the process. Some of the things that you need to make sure to get when you are looking for supplies include:

- Zip ties
- Cables
- Duct tape
- A Raspberry Pi device that is able to run Python
- Battery pack
- A GPRS or GSM module that has audio outlets an dan antenna
- Touch screen
- Velcro squares
- Electrical switch
- Mircophone
- Headphones

- A foam board that has been cut down to be the size of your Raspberry Pi
- 5 VC DC-DC converter
- Sim card

Make sure that when you are picking out the supplies that you would like to use, you are going with ones that are compatible with your device. There are a lot of cheap and imitation options out there, but you want to make sure that you are going with ones that fit with the device and will work well for a long time without breaking.

Once all of the supplies are ready to go, you should make sure that the software and everything else is on the Raspberry Pi 3. Python should be downloaded and installed at this point, especially if you were doing a few of the projects from before, and you also need to take the time to make sure that the Wirehunt option and the Piphone software are in place on the Pi device so that the program goes a bit better. Your first step is going to be to get all of these apps and software over to the Pi device, through your SD card, so they are in place when we get started.

After you have some time to get the software in place and ready to go, you will need to connect the battery over to the switch so that the device has some power to it. Once the battery is connected with the switch, you will be able to connect everything over to your GSM module. Now it is time to take the header of the GSM and connect it over with the converter you have for DC-DC. Now you can link this with the Pi device with one of the excess cables that we asked you to bring. And for a final step, your device needs to be connected, using some more of these extra cables, from your transmit pins so that it is together with the GSM module. A good way to make sure that you are doing this right is to check to see if the pins are connected to the Rx and the Tx ports. After you have all of these in the right spots, it is time to insert your sim card.

So far we have spent time trying to get all the cables connected properly into the modules and the Pi device, but now it is time to assemble all the parts. To make this happen, take your foam board and put the Pi device over it. Your Velcro squares will help, as well as some duct tape, to help you to connect the module, switch, and converter of the GSM to the opposite side of your foam. Make sure to place the battery pack somewhere that it fits between the screen and the Pi device, but don't allow this to be turned to the opposite side for too long since this has a habit of getting really hot.

At this point, you should notice that the parts are basically ready for you to turn them on and let them be used. You just need to take the time to turn on your new "phone" and then dial the numbers that you would like to use. This version is a pretty simple one for you to use and it is pretty much just able to make and maybe receive a few calls for you. As you learn more about using the Raspberry Pi 3, you will be able to make it do a bit more, such as go online, send texts, and so much more. But for now, this is a good project to get some experience in and create a very basic phone.

While you may have started this chapter assuming that it was going to be really hard to get your own phone up and running, you can see that the steps are pretty simple. You just need to get the right supplies and make sure that the software is added to the Pi device from the beginning. Once that is in place, it is about adding on the right wires and putting the parts in place before you are able to make your first call. It is simple and easy to do and you will love how much you are able to add to this simple phone if you would like to down the road.

Conclusion

Thank for making it through to the end of *Raspberry Pi 3: The Ultimate User Guide to Getting Started with Raspberry Pi 3*, let's hope it was informative and able to provide you with all of the tools you need to achieve your goals whatever it may be.

The next step is to pick out the Raspberry Pi 3 device that you would like to use and the project that is the most appealing to you and to get started! This guidebook has provided you with the information that you need to finally get started with coding and computer sciences in a way that is nonthreatening and can actually give you some good results (in the form of the projects that you are working on), all in the same place.

Inside this guidebook, we went from start to finish with the Raspberry Pi 3 to make sure that we are able to get it started, get the right operating system on it, and to make sure that the settings are all in the place that we want them. After doing some of the setup work, we moved on to creating a few projects, ones that you can work on yourself for fun or to get a little bit of practice, such as the home automation system and even a gaming box.

There are so many great projects that you are able to work on when it comes to the Raspberry Pi 3 and anyone will be able to find one that they enjoy and are excited about completing. This guidebook is a great way to teach you how to do some of these projects and to get you started on the right foot with the Raspberry Pi 3.

Finally, if you found this book useful in anyway, a review on Amazon is always appreciated!

www.ingramcontent.com/pod-product-compliance
Lightning Source LLC
Chambersburg PA
CBHW061031050326
40689CB00012B/2769